These Are My Senses

What Can I See?

Joanna Issa

Heinemann LIBRARY

Chicago, Illinois

Edited by Siân Smith
Designed by Richard Parker and Peggie Carley
Picture research by Tracy Cummins
Production by Victoria Fitzgerald
Originated by Capstone Global Library Ltd

Library of Congress Cataloging-in-Publication Data
Cataloging-in-publication information is on file with the Library of Congress.
ISBN 978-1-4846-0431-1 (paperback)
ISBN 978-1-4846-0444-1 (eBook PDF)

Image Credits
Getty Images: Jason Todd, 14, Joanne Wastchak, 16, Jose Luis Pelaez Inc, 15, kirin_photo, cover; Minden Pictures: Suzi Eszterhas, 9; Shutterstock: Colorapt Entertainment, 8, CreativeNature.nl, 18, 21 (right), back cover, Darren Foard, 17, 21 (left), DenisNata, 7, Joop Snijder Photography, 4, Jordache, 13, 22 left, jurra8, 11, 22 (right), Luboslav Tiles, 12, 20 (right), Maxim Kulko, 19, Mogens Trolle, 10, Rik6230, 5, Zorandim, 6, 20 (left)

Every effort has been made to contact copyright holders of material reproduced in this book. Any omissions will be rectified in subsequent printings if notice is given to the publisher.

Contents

What Can I See? 4

Quiz: Opposite Pairs 20

Picture Glossary 22

Index 22

Notes For Teachers
and Parents 23

In This Book 24

What Can I See?

Look at the dog.

The dog runs fast.

Look at the hedgehog.

The hedgehog is spiky.

Look at the leopard.

The leopard has spots.

Look at the zebra.

The zebra has **stripes**.

Look at the rock.

The rock is **smooth**.

Look at the slide.

The slide is twisty.

Look at the elephant.

The elephant is big.

Look at the mouse.

The mouse is small.

Quiz: Opposite Pairs

Can you find opposite pairs?

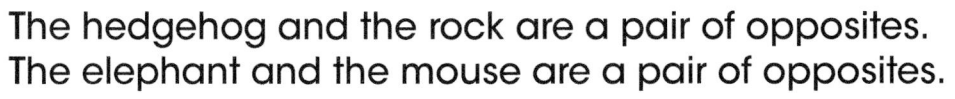

21 The hedgehog and the rock are a pair of opposites.
The elephant and the mouse are a pair of opposites.

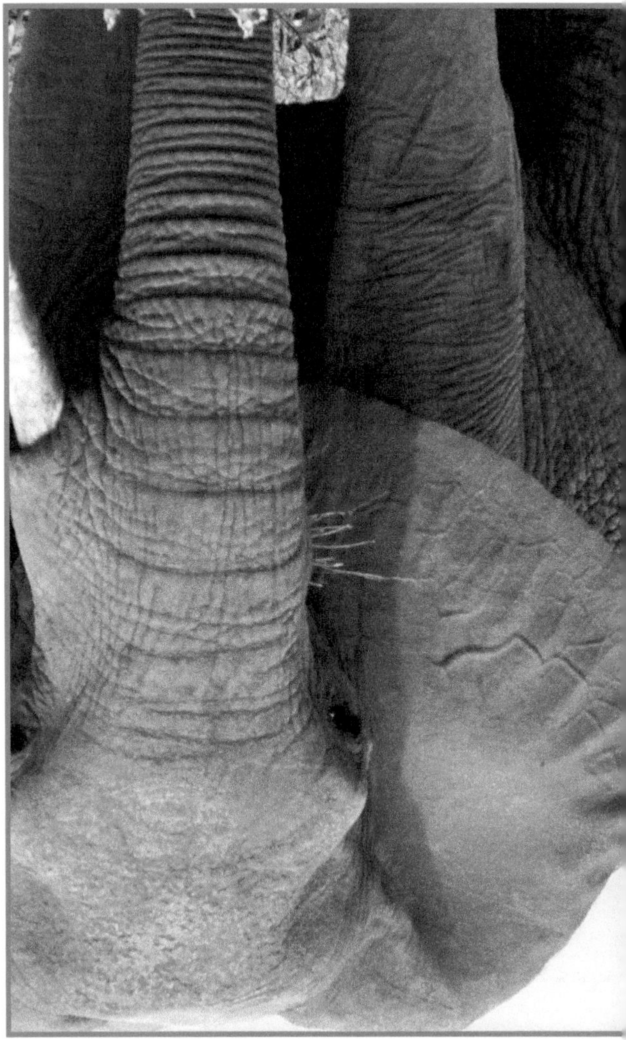

Picture Glossary

 smooth

 stripes

Index

dog 4, 5

elephant 16, 17

hedgehog 6, 7

leopard 8, 9

mouse 18, 19

rock 12, 13

slide 14, 15

zebra 10, 11

Notes For Teachers and Parents

BEFORE READING

Building background:

Ask children what animals they can see near their homes or school.

AFTER READING

Recall and reflection:

Where would children see an elephant? (in a zoo, on TV, in a book) Where would children see a mouse? (in a garden, at a pet store)

Sentence knowledge:

Ask children to look at page 4. Can they see a capital letter? What punctuation mark is at the end of the sentence? Why is it there?

Word knowledge (phonics):

Encourage children to point at the word *big* on page 17. Sound out the three phonemes in the word *b/i/g*. Ask children to sound out each phoneme as they point at the letters and then blend the sounds together to make the word *big*. Challenge them to say some words that rhyme with *big*. (dig, fig, pig)

Word recognition:

Have children point to the word *slide* on page 14. Can children find it again on page 15?

EXTENDING IDEAS

Play "I Spy." Say, "I spy with my little eye something beginning with the sound ..." (say the starting phoneme of an object in the room). Invite children to guess what the object might be. If they choose something beginning with the chosen sound (but it is not the correct object) say, "Yes, ... does begin with ... but that's not what I spy." When a child guesses the object, then he or she takes a turn at choosing something to spy that the others must guess.

In This Book

Topic

sight and senses

Sentence stems

1. Look _____ dog.

2. The rock _____.

3. _____ is small.

High-frequency words

at

has

is

look

the

24